By Pauline Joelle

Written in the fall of 1997, and only recently resumed from the darkest corners of prehistoric hard drives, *The Third World* is a collection of poems that sing about our relation to the natural world and to others. Karalla recollects fleeting fragments of past loves to discover that the value of romance lies not in the everlasting endurance of the illusory beliefs we project on the other, but rather in the overpowering intensity of those transitory yet unforgettable instants. In love, the relation to the other can only be as that to an ancient god; Karalla's poems give us back the haptics, the flavors, and the vivid colors from those fugacious experiences.

In this lived mythology, societal frames are ever-present, and a person outside the moral framework, like "The Third World", easily becomes the object of miscast prejudice. But she doesn't care about the bigotry or the self-righteous rituals surrounding her, nor about the misinformed disapproval of a potential loved one. She continues to follow her own morals, and strives to remain in "The Third World", freer, outside the other worlds, unveiling hypocrisy, but always with an open mind. Starting from her childhood, and unfolding through the lights and sounds of maritime landscapes and of NYC's *beau monde*, *The Third World* is Karalla's polysemous hymn to life.

CONTENTS

Introduction

My writing career began at the age of ten.
They were letters of suicide to my dear Stepmother, a mother of two — now three. Only one month (and my stepmother) divided my new brother and me. One day, a mother of 11 children asked me whether my brother or I had skipped a grade or been left behind. I said, "No". Looking puzzled, she asked our months of birth. I looked squarely at her and said, "we're twins, but I was a month late."
Her mouth became an O.

O, how rational life becomes in youth.
We attended Catholic School and 9:00 a.m. Mass each Sunday on account of my father. My once-divorced stepmother was denied the Sacred Host along with my once-divorced father, because they were living in SIN. That changed with the death of my father. Now, my less sinful stepmother sashayed past her neighbors to receive the Sacred Host. My world changed, too. New house, new neighbors — same old questions.

One night, we watched a late-night horror film on our old television in our new house. I refused to look at the gory details of death, which landed me in the cold dark basement with the fresh fingerprints of my stepmother on the lock of the door. I stayed awake the entire night, Praying to God for the Sun to appear.
My future penance was scrubbing the copper pots to a shiny gold each day.

O, there was more. My penned pleas to my stepmother for a quick death began. After all the notes and no replies, I took my writing career on the road. Some in life end happily ever after. I no longer pray for death, but to live each day to the fullest. And She, of course, goes to 9:00 a.m. Mass every Sunday to receive the Sacred Host.

BLASPHEMY

In New York, I live in one world and the other
I try desperately to stay outside.
But if you always keep an open mind, you won't close the door before having entered.
You've arrived when you've realized that "the North had lost the War".

As you stand between the pages of Architectural Digest, in strict attire,
Noses wave high that mimic apples stuck in the tides,
Bobbing their way
methodologically
in search of shores to land recognition.

Bodies float in a current of drinks, sufficing each other,
Like boats seeking a lighthouse signal
To nightly dock themselves in jetties of flesh,
To prince their dreams until the morning wakes.

Women having fallen flawlessly from the billboards that rocket over 42nd,
and   In an astute manner,
Know that "Down to Earth" means *Grungy Rock & Rollers*".

As you sit for dinner,
The pressure to hold your fork so correctly,
— which I do naturally — but so grand a pressure!,
I can't help but purposely fumble,
To hold my fork in a way that has never been done before,
It's my only hope to stop the urge to fly my fork through an air of accidents,
In order to break the monotonous reformed mechanical habit,
So that maybe in the form of eating,
a taste may be acquired.

To work so hard to mirror skyscrapers and not humans,
Sends the breaking point of Dr. Jekyll & Mr. Hyde
To live within and not succumb to such an ordained ritual,
One can't help Blasphemy from occurring,
In-just to save nature's core within,
To escape — what we call civilization.

ELEPHANT'S POST

He salutes first, on the combat post
then he conquered my chair, demanding me host
in a lieutenant sprinkle, stood Zorba the God,
with a cockeyed face, pocketing golden pods

Once more to meet, I picketed the chair
a renegade laugh jointed the air
we inhabited the diplomatic sea
where Captain Elephants pee.

The voluntary heart blinded the sight
and a signature of mud, tabloid the right
we dropped in arms, a principal truce
to render a priest, for the sleepy blue hearse.

Lie here my darling, in wars of sun charms
under spaghetti trees, commands no harms.

MOON BALM

We patch-worked our faces,
to relinquish concrete places.
Fingers smeared the lips in green,
platform roles of King & Queen.

As authors we crowned the Plaka,
to knight the air a harpoon crackle.
The lure designates, "Moon Balm,"
as the audience applaud the palm.

Then motors, rewrote the roads to Matala,
As victory ruled passages of papa.
Crowds profiled in cast of cream wonder,
inscribing glory in reflections thunder.

Rejoicing sonnets notes the core,
we Broadway the spirit's flight in score.
As yellow tongues sing "No master, No slave,"
Hair sprayed youths hailed "Alive & Brave."

Native passion churned to the beat of drums,
To star in Moon Balm, free to succumb.

KIND DANGER

Lay me promise, to sleep,
The green machine weeps,
Boy, play me that tune,
I'm a kind danger, coming to you.

Now powder puff me up to cue,
I topple in the mesh of you,
Breathe in the frontiers, of your hair,
Vibrant Senor, I precooked the lair.

You lithographed me basil,
Then banked a loaf of witch hazel,
Splurging the domestic dole down,
My verging purple cow.

Letter footprints of your lips,
Pumpkins liberty on my hips,
To inherent ruffles in mind,
A portraiture hairpins this time.

The moon solar in blind,
To fennel the passage you drive,
Intuition hounds in sap,
The frozen food sets the trap.

ECLIPSE

I love you so
that I could die
but your eyes
turned away from mine.

I asked you why
and you replied
it's your physique
I will never seek.

But I, Diane am
of the moon
as you are, Apollo
of the sun.

And so it is
you said so sad
but I inside
can only love a man.

I loved him so.
I would surely die
so I made a change
from girl to guy.

You laughed and smiled
and held my hand
said you truly love
you silly Diane.

TRUE GLUE

As I lie here in my fishnet glue
I dream of You where your eyes are blue
and You chained me tight with your lips so red.
I watched You close and sang purple thoughts, instead.

You laughed in tickle and jumped on a beat.
I sat at your toes and painted your feet.
You lifted me up to the shade of the moon.
Your smile was blowing the sun in tune

So I bleached my hair green for You to see
and You hiked your eyes and wished upon a tree
I sat oceaned to what your dream might be
so You opened your eyes where they swam so blue
You smiled and said *"we are so true"*

THE MARK

I shifted the strainer to see the Mark
Time of pigments, the pigment's of the heart.
Once my soul held only Diamond tears
but now it's fresh with the sun so mere.

I heard your horse roar with the loons
as we laid in the shadow of tunes
Your face was naked in the purple day
my body was pink with mustard to play.

You held your hand so high above mine
and pulled me from the depths of Hades so kind
but the light went dim and I could not see
the color of pigments that fell from the tree.

SONIC BOOM

The metacarpus spreads its organ,
Into a wing of fraternal light,
Blinding the Gods into a slumber murk,
To ordain Eros's "Sonic Boom".

Beginning:

Lovers, Constellations, Eyes,
But, their Formica cohabitation,
Which formatted their presoak passion,
Freckled love into a cursory fluster,
Their felicity orchestrates,
Into the gauche silence that forsakes,
Ophelia, oceaned in muse,
To the openhanded current,
While the plagued cavalier,
Cavorts in a kerosene hue.

¡STOP!

The improvised meters woke the Gods,
Vermicelli rained a tapestry,
As the Gods lost their appetite,
For Eros's day to be insane.

MONKEY WRENCH LOVE

I woke within a wreckage of existence
That spoke of their core oceaned within,
A man voiced his crusade and laid his claim
To love all measurable things that habit
a biscuit hell or an orange tree heaven.

While wheeling his tongue in a sonorous rap,
Hermetic horizons reined the crooked sky
That penetrated the innocent womb of thyme
In the fluid filter flesh that powders the soul
We embark upon a crouton montage door,
Wood planks plagued the empty place in shrine
My eyes fall hostage to the gilded crib inside.

There laid Love Monkey conducting her resume
To orchestrate her parsley wings into a Xerox note,
Out of Love the Monarch clips her rosary will
To resolute a prison of his mistress Monkey's thrills.
She laid as a harbored serf altered and buttered
in a roomette coffin toasted at dinner.

Then shuffleboard feet arose in unpronounced time,
As queuing crowds poured in consomme rime,
Their eyes glazing stones in silicone bones
announcing the final signature of the Roman Rodeo.
Marrowing words, unharnessed the foreclosure of Monkey's demise,
Irate in heel, I forbade this merriment requiem
as the Master transmits his sonic echo,
"It's the currency of Love's Lottery."

The bedlam sat in looking glass frame, cymbal and overexposed,
In a crux plea a voice is heard, "Croquet Anyone."

UMBRA

In a union command of one,
Dramas the eclipse of man & woman,
Why love in windshield passion reins,
Inhibit the innate midst of pain.

To shadow flowers the breath we breathe,
Laws the riders blind to see,
Just to suffice an illusion,
That dons the spirits conclusion.

BAD GIRL

Souling the religious intoxicating colors upon her head,
Her hair canvasses the truth
which paints the brownout of the innate.

Her buttonhole entrance, in her liberty attire,
Tailspins the guests at the white table cloth occasion

into a curbside stand,
With their heads hedging
in a sonorous mathematical plural state.

While the magnesia row of passer-
buyers final trim their milkman eyes,
Elbows quickly converse from the rosebud maidens,
To the investigation of Bad Girl's entourage of men.

The roses close their petals in disappointment,
To plumb the point of non homogenized bank$,
to Romance the evenings in Mink.

The cockpit opens a hard-boiled conversation,
The coefficients engage her in an eloquent
dental coffee cake ingredient verse,
she exits a billow laugh as the word "Proust"
promenades from her misconstrued lips.

The ever omniscient humble host
enters the ring of the pasture pit,
Entertaining himself with dreams of her
He moors his composite posture of authority,

Airing his vocal cords for the pre-formatted passage,
To tongue the punctuated articulated words,
that would magistrate a doting command
Of her Robust attention.

Clearing his recipe throat
so that each word would unsaddle itself
in a perfect pitch of intonation,

as the words rise and fall in his head,
so does the vision of her.
He cradles the captured thought,

as he waits for the lunar class moment
to interject the fiber sonnet,
To render her
in awe of him.

He views the sentence train coming from the present speaker,
he sees the Caboose
and knows that the voice will soon demise in a Period,

BUT

the speaker Commas,

as his words escaped with accelerated speed that intersected the speakers
words which resulted in a cowerofleftovermashedgoulash.
She retorts a look at him and jeers

"WHAT?"

He tries to retain his crabgrass demure,
as his lips crayon the lobster death squeal "Eeeeeeeee-quaaality."

"Equality" she repeats,

In her noteworthy stand and continues;
"Yes we are all equal, we all take a shit each day and
those that don't are constipated?"

As she excuses herself to the ladies room.

MASTER PRINCE ABATED

He sits alone at night inside,
Doing his thing which he must hide,
For all would cast an ugly eye,
If they knew what he did with his thing.

So alone he sits with no girl in mind,
To bring flowers lie down by her side,
The truth to him holds deep within,
So he won't lie in trying to pretend.

All ye women from all around,
Listen to these words that make you cringe,
Here is a Prince that Masturbates,
Cause he loves so dearly, he can wait.

So bow to him and make him bread,
For this man is honest to the end,
He will be happy all the way,
If you don't judge him at his play.

BLACK KING

These radicals are free
to move with ease
bouncing so kind
with color in mind
adventures individual
but clearly visual
structures may differ
no radical is sure
on a canvas, we can survive
in the same space, we thrive.

THE THIRD WORLD

THIRD WORLD: Those countries not allied with the communist or non communist bloc. Bloc: A group of persons, states, or nations, united by common interest.
(The concise American Heritage Dictionary/Houghton Mifflin)

SOCIALLY: This country's ideas are uncommon to the social blocs. Union to a bloc, just for social acceptance or security, would subject the country's submissiveness to populating sky-scrapers and to boring superhighways eradicating the old back roads. This country may lack in modern materialist items that the blocs offer, but this country is too rich to be convinced of what one needs not. Socially independent, she stands to be controversial & socially unaccepted. But as Mistress, for the mere Ownership of Self, many travel a great distance to share in the history and knowledge of "Her" development.

POLITICALLY: For this country to be sitting defenselessly alone and unaligned with a bloc. Blocs inhabit Her to show their power in the form of flowers or wrath, with the objective to attain a marriage between the two countries. The bloc offers protection from other blocs that may try and re-enter her shores. To concord with a bloc, she will agree to support the bloc's political interests, contribute in the great ARMS race and surrender the right to freely advocate for Herself.

CULTURALLY: She is free of Matrimony with a bloc. She has wide open fields for the wild spirit to cross streams, climb mountains and nourish thy-self in a verbatim of birth. The arts pour, the same as a spring that opens & falls, caressing gently the mountains to feed the hungry in the valleys. The presence of old souls float as Gods with wings to balance the internal forces, so that the heart relinquishes its own voice, Free, just as the wild spirited stallion of the virgin terrain, unattached to the social realm, his mane blowing with ease in the wind, without reins or rider to guide for he alone knows himself, verbatim, as this country is his, it's "Her" equal.

This is for the Mind of those who have never traveled to "THE THIRD WORLD" and don't know the fruits "She" bears.

MALDOROR

I, a monk on distant sands,
Hear the songs from unknown bands,
Lost in passages that echo in dreams,
Shadowing the sea, I scream,

"MALDOROR"

I want to lie in the belly of the beast,
Place my soul at his feet,
I'll rip my heart from my chest,
As you accept nature's core without jest,

"MALDOROR"

Embrace me warm with your cold truth,
Billboard Heroes empty to soothe,
The pyramid slaves a bow in prayer,
And all along, there is no God to care,

"MALDOROR"

I lie beached, naked upon the thorns,
For a thousand years, solo and alone,
I await you to enter the shores,
To accompany me to the mores,

"MALDOROR"

Les Chants de Maldoror (The Songs of Maldoror) is a French poetic novel, or a long prose poem. It was written and published between 1868 and 1869 by the Comte de Lautréamont.

LADY IN WAITING

In a cake blue veneer face
Ghost glacier breast in place
Her hands naked in empty crust
As dreams repent, sparkle dust.

As she waits

For the remainder of time to pair
She sits shrouded in the Human Chair
That contorts her limbs in a cocoon
Demising her unlicensed passion.

As she waits

Thoughts tick-tock in uterus silence,
While Mother's juggernaut springs time
Her ghetto belly generates only angst,
She remorses in a vermilion freezer, Thanx!

As she waits

In a disarray received she chides with man,
Unknowingly she fertilized the webbed pan
To wade in fairy tales of Princes,
That banked dreams to eschew the senses.

As she waits

For herself, Astute in shatterproof stand,
To lease liberty in flatware understanding
To flick the social shaver of Human air
To Certify herself outside Her Chair.

ZELDA

The aura of Zelda dances Sight
we hail her our North Star of Plight
she stirs the blind awake in discourse
and accepts the 'Wild Spirited Horse.'

All in hem relinquish their hearts
for the parent of patience, beauties the Mark
as they liberate their souls to open
and emerge into thy-self, flee the den.

Mother Zelda threads branches of race
that orchids glory in hearts place
she bids actively to spring world peace
to reason brothers & sisters to rise equally

A white African explorer, she
searching the realms for women chiefs
to sister the social plow in pledge
and obstruct rites in the power of knowledge.

As podium speakers pocket her "Feminist"
she retorts, "No, I'm a Humanist"
I'm the daughter of my Mother's power
and happy to orbit her light, that Towers.

ODILE

Odile is the star
in her own film on Mars
crowds & flowers at her feet
while only two she will take your seat

She has eyes of black & hair to match
and walks the command of wrath
with arms in motion, she snows the beast
Enthralling all my piccolo niece

When her mood is a bit down
all ears find shelter across town
her cries won't let you forget
she's not quite happy yet

We wonder if it comes with her name
for Odile is very sane
it's us adults that quiver in strain
because we can't hold her reins

She reminds me of myself
when my family would scream help
I know her Mother well
and this is just the beginning I can tell.

FLAT TIRES

Matisse fell subserviently odd in flowers
while the succulent Cinderella unleashes her power
Your opposite Sun Apollo applauds orchards in the Mo.
Being sidetracked the bus faithfully devours my toe.

In a faint fever I shuttle the social thoughts
to excavate the satire norm floundering a wrought
but everyday thrust knew highways of sirens
that halts in the parent search of flat tires.

THE CURRENT GOD

Summons surf me at an angle
Resonating eschewed senses in a mangle
Suffrage plugs the current God
Surging Soul to verge in mind in sod

Thoughts meters a pilgrim's physique
Mistress' ears transforms to Sultana's conceit
Avenue seeds taste in construed sound
Pilot aromas render in needles bound

Penning white suffices as inherent sleep
Relinquished hearts leafed open in reap
Razing reasons of native un-timed wake
Miring the mere current God's rake.

UNTITLED

He had big feet
little teeth
and a mole
to go bye

Some sang
others cried
while he stood
to feel a line

A day in May
where flowers came
he watched the stone
where water froze

On the beach
his feathered friend
went and spoke
a spring in time

I love you me
and words can't tell
this lovely lie
shall never be

and when you know
the story more
you shall go
and be a toad

I dreamt this
as my heart kissed
the lilac tree
of my sweet prince

NEXT

Oh, distant moon
in quiet tune
the earth is mad
and I am sad

So off in flight
with all this blight
to darken your smile
for many a mile

I wonder in time
of neither yours nor mine
but the children ahead
where all will be said

In years before
we closed the door
there was a near Moon
that danced with a spoon

But the people were mad
and destroyed what they had
so now it is said
we can read about it instead.

MUSES'

My madness eludes me
but the scape I see
down by the sun,
where the mocking hums
threads my orange brain
as the sea winds wane
the sparkle of Mother's edge
drips clocks singing Red
As I sit 'neath the Rock
chewing words to dock
The Muses' silent rhyme
plays shadows in mime
as night chimes trees
plucking strings of me.

SIMPLE SHELL SKIN

Beauty on shore
waiting in door
pebbles turn dust
time smells must

Sun rains Black
whispers swing back
Moon wash Gold
bright lights told

Third Sight home
back along roam
Heart beat Red
Truth pour Said

Simple Shell Skin
ready crawl in
Travel down hall
where one is all

Pen closed hand
open your fan
No control line
sings so fine.

FLOWERS

As your belly turns in lie
the cancer eats you inside.
You pray that lord to die
as your face seeks to hide
this shame, inherent sin
passed through ages of kin.
Why must we pretend
Is the Truth not the end
No, it is the beginning of time
where our friendship shines
and flowers hold their color
of want to be no other.

COUP de GRACE

In solemn Hosanna he computes
and exploits his theory of solipsism
His conservative corn syrup charisma
helmets his chanticleer demure
So he flowers the lovelorn lobotomy
of his phantom courtship's
This hierarchy soul hermits himself
to solicit the Virgin soil
The intoxication's of Mary
spots intermissions of soft-ware
Planting himself in The New Testament
he awaits the dark to conclave his flower
And knowing the coquetting Houris would fall
intimately on with a crucifying hex
He pulls the sausage stamen to solar
the flaccid into a copyright.

He honeymoons the stigma in a dexterous coup de grace.

CURTSY

Your offbeat gesture relishes in grin,
Waning the reverence your soul in pun,
Bending your knees with one foot forward,
You raise the Holy Water to alert the Happy Hour,
A satire facade hibernates in fluster,
As the sublet society beckons acceptance.

CONCERTO EPILOGUE

In a flat wrought turn, The Third World fell beneath me,
While voices of unknown bands kettle a merriment requiem,
I construed the trinity that meters the un-sonnet injuries.

My hair the canvas of color, that would sink eyes in
a traffic jam of rubber-necking for the mere sake of fun,
Is now black with the wrath of mud.

The butter of my humble lips that melt green into my love,
Crowning the Moon Balm nights, now laid un-soft
in crimson, nursing the fluids of red.

I raise the metacarpus that once held Blasphemy in a fork,
In the communion with Mother Earth's grammar,
The skinless bones winged in slang, "gravel".

The summit juggernauts the Sonic Boom, that contorts
my limbs to insinuate a confession, "Forgive me Father",
My miscarried legs now lie flat in limbo custard CURTSY.

The blaring sun miniskirts my sight of the firsthand accounts
of my demonic attire, the broken & unbroken threads
orchestrate the diary of my wraps that titles "War of the Roads."

In a Simple Shell Skin, I lie eclipsed with the Gods,
To liquidate in dust with Love Monkey and Maldoror,
In a Kind Danger, the ushering Muses embryo my spirit by unction.

I register mischance ministry, and edifice the Cracy of Self,
To morsel the fall, and in a Coup de Grace,
my lattice soul lauds the catalogued appendage, "HALE."

A frozen lift erects my bike to a drawing jump start,
The motor kicks, while the investigating engines roar
to shadow my screams, "I SO DIRTY."